THE LIGHT BEYOND DARKNESS

Verses of the Heart, Mind, and Cosmos

STANLEY COUTINHO

Dedication

To my godson, Caleb Anthony Gomindes—
This book is a piece of me, just as you are a piece of my
heart.
May these words remind you that life is poetry—
even in its chaos, even in its quiet.
May you always find your own voice, your own rhythm,
and your own meaning in this world.

To those who have shaped me—
your presence, your love, and even your absences
have carved these lines into existence.
Every lesson, every moment, every scar—
this book holds them all.

And to you, the reader—
these pages are yours now.
May you find something here that lingers,
something that makes you feel a little less alone.

Preface

This book is a collection of moments—some fleeting, some etched in time. Each poem is a frame, a heartbeat, a breath caught between memory and imagination. I write because words refuse to stay silent, because feelings demand motion, because life itself is poetry in motion.

These verses are fast-paced, cinematic—snapshots of love, loss, resilience, and wonder. They are meant to be felt, not just read. To linger, like the final notes of a song or the last light of dusk before night claims the sky.

Some of these words are for me, some for you, and some for a boy named Caleb Anthony Gomindes. He will grow up in a world of stories, and perhaps, somewhere in these pages, he will find his own reflection—his own spark.

This book is not just poetry. It's a journey. A conversation. A piece of me, given to you.

Take your time. Let the words move you. And when you close this book, may you carry something more than when you first opened it.

Acknowledgements

This book is a journey—one shaped by love, loss, and the fleeting beauty of moments. I could not have walked this path alone.

To my godson, Caleb Anthony Gomindes—you are a light in my life, and this book is, in part, for you. May you always find wisdom in words and strength in your own voice.

To my father, Domingos Caetano Lyndon Cesar Judas Coutinho—because of you, I started reading at a very young age. What began as simple words on a page soon grew into a lifelong habit, compounding into a world of imagination, stories, and poetry. Your love for knowledge shaped mine, and for that, I am forever grateful.

To my mother, Maria de Lourdes Espectação Couto—your unwavering belief in me, even without fully understanding the depths of my creative journey, has been one of my greatest sources of strength. In your quiet support, I found the freedom to explore, to dream, and to become.

To my brothers, Ryan and Raymond, and my sister, Lavita—thank you for being a part of my lifelong journey. Your presence has always brought strength, love, and comfort.

To my sister-in-law, Cheryl Pereira—your warmth and kindness have made our family stronger. Your support means more than words can express, and I'm grateful for the love and joy you bring.

To Flavia Pereira and family—our bond as close family friends has been a source of warmth and support. Thank you for always being there.

To my dear friends:

Valencia Rodrigues, a special and close friend, and the mother of my godson—thank you for being part of this journey from the very beginning. Your presence in my life has been a blessing.

Conrad Rodrigues, my best friend—thank you for your steady support and unwavering presence throughout my life.

Vinayak Sherekar—your constant friendship, kindness, and encouragement have meant the world to me.

Newton Cardozo—your steady belief in my journey and voice has been a constant source of strength.

Dianne Dorado, my best friend from the Philippines—thank you for being the first to recognize the depth of my potential and for always seeing beyond the surface.

Charress Posecion, also from the Philippines—you were the one who first saw my passion for poetry and cherished it. Your encouragement helped me see what was possible.

Rajan Cardozo—for being a constant, supportive presence.

Malagoda Francis, my first friend from Sri Lanka—our bond formed during my first career sailing in the waters of Malaysia. That instant connection will always be close to my heart.

Saddam Sounshi—your friendship and belief have been a source of strength, and I'm grateful for your presence in my life.

John Gomes and Stanley Rodrigues my childhood friends —thank you for walking beside me from the earliest days.

Akhil Moopnar—your friendship continues to mean a great deal to me.

Mohsin Xec, my dear friend—thank you for your companionship, your support, and the sincerity you've always brought into our friendship.

To every poet, storyteller, and artist who has ever dared to bare their soul—I stand on your shoulders.

And to you, the reader—thank you for allowing my words into your world. May they find you at the right time, in the right way.

With deep gratitude,

Stanley Coutinho

1. Whispers of Faith

Feels like you're here, feels like you're gone,
A fleeting shadow, yet holding on.
I make myself believe you're near,
A whispered prayer, a hope sincere.

Was it you who led me through?
A guiding light, a hidden clue.
My body ages, my heart stays bright,
Lost in memories, chasing light.

So many faces, masks to see,
So many voices silencing me.
Yet wisdom grows within my mind,
A quiet strength, a truth to find.

Getting closer feels so right,
Like rivers flowing soft and light.
Yet heartbreak lingers, wounds still stay,
But faith will never fade away.

2. The Thousandth Prayer

I just woke up
from the hangover of my last trail
a hammer pounding in my mind,
but it won't last, like fleeting lust.

I open the window,
let the awakening rise,
where sunflowers sway in golden fields,
and smiles meet their worthy prize.

I run toward my beliefs,
striking hard, reaching high,
chasing the purest rush
the euphoria of being alive.

I pray to you,
let me rest in your refuge,
for I have searched
a thousands times.

3. I Forgive to Not Forget

Say it or don't—a spell is cast,
A curse that lingers, shadows past.
I'd acknowledge, even pretend,
To show you trust too firm to bend.

Trusted you like a mirror of self,
Broken trust shattered in betrayal's stealth.
Walking out from the scripted show,
Playing the puppet of someone I know.

Guilt unveils truth in a cosmic sign,
Granting me chances, again and again,
Though it fractured my earnest prime.
Lessons learned with every dime
No stone left unturned in time.

I forgive, but not to forget,
Only to walk ahead—no regret.

4. Tides of Letting Go

I don't wanna hold you back,
leave you in a memory of goldfish.
Please don't turn back to me,
breaking me in tears.

I put my hand in silver sand,
clasping the tiny granules,
watching them slip away,
escaping the time we held so close.

But I say to myself
I had the best time of my life.

Feeling so high, feeling so low,
caught between the spark of light.
I gave myself to you.

I run toward the seashore,
to drench in the high tides of happiness,
only to realize
nothing lasts forever.

5. Geometric Love

I run towards you,
but life feels uneven.

Please, square up my world
make it steady, make it right.

I don't want to fall into a love triangle,
where someone always gets left behind,
or the stillness of a cornered angle,
forgotten, unmoved.

I just want the circle of bare minimum,
where things are simple, where love is enough.
To rest at its center balanced, cherished,
never standing at the edge.
Yet even circles can become cages,
spinning endlessly, keeping us bound.

But maybe love isn't meant to fit a shape,
not angles to measure or lines to trace.
Maybe it's motion fluid, expanding,
finding its form in the space we create.

6. Glory Through Surrender

With a will, I stand again,
hunger sharp within my mind.
I seek the path to thrive
with patience and pride, I abide.

I walk through the jungle's roar,
bringing forth the best in me.
I slay the pride of the lion,
with patience in my mind.

A collective decision
precise execution it arrives.

I turn back to my nest,
with the prize of the evening kill,
leaving behind hatred and revenge,
in the eyes of their newborn to survive.

One must survive
in the battle of hope.
One must doom
in the battle of surrender to thrive.

7. The Awakening

Hell of a ride,
I took you along with me.
The journey was hard to break from
but somehow, I stopped.

Wind wavered across my battered face,
a cool sigh of relief by the afterpass.
It told me:
Don't play with the fire of a stranger.

It burned so deep,
cut so hard
but I pulled myself out,
awakened the awakening
with closed eyes wide open.

Gunshots echoed loud,
shattering the useless buzz.
Maybe this was the lesson
to never fall
into the black and blue abyss again.

8. Face the Fear

Fond of fear,
I swim through tears.
I rise, I face the mirror
Never to veer, never to disappear.

Shadows chase, but I don't break,
Echoes whisper, yet I don't shake.
Through the storm, I carve my way
A rebel of night, a child of day.

I drift to sleep,
Dare to dream,
Dare to scream
Not from fear,
Not for the dear,
But for a conscience clear.

9. The Last Battleground

Going to the front,
Fighting through day and night,
Promised to come back home,
But I feel so alone.

My mind spins round and round
Battleground! Battleground!
Battleground! Battleground!

Every ambush, every fight,
Pulls me deeper to the ground.
I am falling asleep,
Take me in your arms.

You were the first I chose to love,
The one I swore to fight beside
Until my last breath.

Please take me home, if you find me alive.
Please take me to grave, if you find me dead.

Bury me inside her heart,
Seal my fate with love inside out.

I don't want war.
I don't want love.
Not anymore.

Battleground! Battleground!
Battleground! Battleground!

10. Lost in the Night

Maybe it wasn't you
I've been turning to.
Maybe it wasn't you
I've been longing for.

You took me for granted in my own home,
Yet I kept holding on.
Sipped my youth away,
Danced beneath the starry nights.

Northern lights and gloomy skies,
I searched for myself in the darkest light.
You have been my driving strength.

I pray to the universal force
Let the bad sink into the filthy ground,
Let the good lift me to the galaxy round.

Maybe now, it all makes sense
Lost in nostalgia and reminiscence.

11. The Silence of the Drive

Tell me which shoes to wear,
which watch to strap
time's slipping,
we're running out.

Tonight, we bolt from the show.
But where are you?
Don't come if you're late.
Come fast we're heading north,
our place to breathe,
our heaven on earth.

I park in the chaos
party mess,
smokers in a trance,
daddy's girls in high heels,
money burning in the trash.

I steady my mind,
head against the wall,
spinning solo,
feet losing ground.

But I come back hard,

leave it all behind
high on the silence
of the drive.

Alone.
Never returning,
never chasing
the wild,
the reckless,
the crazy prey.

12. I Create No Time

14

I sleep in my dreams,
drifting beyond time.

Radiate and vibrate
a whisper of light,
rippling sound to the distant universe.

I appear to the new world,
careless, weightless, boundless.

I want to live asound
not to run or fall,
no bounds, no confines.

I create no time,
only motion, only sound.

13. A Prayer at Dawn, A Whisper at Dusk

I rest with gratitude, soft and deep,
Drifting gently into sleep.
I wake with prayer upon my lips,
Blessings rising with my fingertips.

I walk with purpose, step by step,
Embracing all with no regret.
I shoulder trials with a smile,
Letting worries fade awhile.

I open my mind to boundless skies,
Yet it longs where joy resides.
I close my mind to restless days,
Yet solitude still calls my name.

I greet the dusk beneath my feet,
Where my soul and silence meet.
And as the night begins to fall,
I wait in peace for morning's call.

14. Season's Dance

Summer sun, burning bright,
Scorching heat, a blinding light.
Strolling down the southern shore,
Rowing kayaks evermore.

Here comes the monsoon rain,
Thunder roars a wild refrain.
Mighty drops in glassy shine,
Getting wet, your hand in mine.

Autumn falls, love drifts away,
Golden leaves in sad decay.
Cooling streams begin to run,
Winter whispers, frost has come.

Frozen ice and penguins glide,
Snowflakes twirl and cold winds chide.
Crackling fires, warm embrace,
Season's dance ends with grace.

15. Whispers of a New Beginning

I want to have a glimpse of you
The soft touch, your smile for no reason.
I just want to look into your eyes,
Beyond words, my tears rolling down.

I want to hold you in every step you take,
Your touchdown, your cracking sound.
I just lay down for you,
You benchmark your footprints on myself.

I burst into laughter, harder than your move.
I wanna stroll down the memory lane,
Whisper the sigh of calm.
Star gazing, moonlight shine,
Wonder world, newborn align.

A pinch of pain, awakening begins,
Hope of mystery unfolds, future awaits.

16. To the Surface, To the Stars

I break free from the bounded ties
Escape to the journey I seek to thrive
Shedding the unspoken mind
I push myself to the surface high

My heart's the same, but it feels young
Memories old, yet still feel gold
The past is gone an unseen cosmic plan
Still to cherish, but my heart pounds on

Through lavender fields, I walk
Through the River Thames, I swim
Past Heathrow skies, I fly
Through dreams, I reach beyond the sky

17. The Last Sunset

Riddle me with your betrayal,
I close my eyes, nothing left to say.
You kill me softly with your kiss,
A final touch I won't dare miss.

I walk away, head held high,
No sorrow left, no need for goodbye.
My ego clings to a crumbling ledge,
Dragged down by ghosts of past regrets.

Hushed steps echo in the night,
Yet in my arms, I hold them tight.
Blushing skies fade from sight,
Never to see the last sunset's light.

Now I rest beneath the moon,
A quiet soul, a fate too soon.

18. Echoes of the Cosmic Dream

Falling back into my dreams,
Falling back into my peace.
In a lonely world of galaxy twins,
I find myself in the echoes of a thousand light-years.

Falling back in the middle of nowhere,
Falling back to the surface of truth.
In a lonely world of galaxy twins,
I find myself in the echoes of a thousand light-years.

Gravity forgets who I am,
A shadow unbound, drifting weightless.
I reach for a leap but space holds me still,
Caught in the hush of mindful sleep.

Rippling sound waves whisper from afar,
Waking me up to a force unseen.
A glimpse of power, divine yet distant
A pulse reminding me, I am not alone.

Falling back in the middle of nowhere,
Falling back into my peace,
Falling back into my dreams.

19. Sailing into the Unknown

Sailing into the open arms of the sea,
with measured steps and near-clash companions
galloping hopes, fresh adventures
caught in the chaos of a story untold.

I bow before the mighty sun drowning,
spilling its brilliance to light our way.
With naked eyes, we wonder.
With sweet tongues, we spell,
longing for the salt-stained air
with every step we sail.

I sleep a night in unseen excitement,
drifting toward the port where my soul can rest.
I seek, I carve the path unknown
drawn to the hope of mystery and insight.

I quench my thirst for the quest,
feeling it pulse in every cell of me.
Back home, I begin again
a new experience unfolding.

20. Nature's Wonder

Waving Rainbow
Down the river hill,
I stand still,
Admiring nature's wonder.

The storm of rain has just passed,
Leaving a trail of colors that last.
Life is a dash of aftermath wonder,
Rising beyond each disastrous blunder.

Nothing remains ever,
Memories immortal forever.
Eyes behold each silent cry,
Every smile I wonder why?

21. Star Fall & The Flower Bloom

The death of a shooting star,
Naked eyes catch its glitter.
A newborn cosmic world ignites,
Spun in a web of galaxy light.

Spacecraft wanders,
Astronauts pray,
Science whispers
As skyfall thunders.

I catch hold of a flower,
Blooming in quiet splendor.
Its essence lingers,
Lasting to its fullest measure.

Karma lets us act and choose,
In every search, we find our truths.